by Iain Gray

Lang**Syne**

PUBLISHING

WRITING *to* REMEMBER

Lang**Syne**

PUBLISHING

WRITING *to* REMEMBER

79 Main Street, Newtongrange,
Midlothian EH22 4NA
Tel: 0131 344 0414   Fax: 0845 075 6085
E-mail: info@lang-syne.co.uk
www.langsyneshop.co.uk

Design by Dorothy Meikle
Printed by Printwell Ltd
© Lang Syne Publishers Ltd 2018

ISBN 978-1-85217-480-4

Baker

MOTTO:
While I have breath I hope
(and)
So run that you may obtain.

CREST:
A naked arm with the hand
holding a swan's head.

Chapter one:

The origins of popular surnames

by George Forbes and Iain Gray

If you don't know where you came from, you won't know where you're going is a frequently quoted observation and one that has a particular resonance today when there has been a marked upsurge in interest in genealogy, with increasing numbers of people curious to trace their family roots.

Main sources for genealogical research include census returns and official records of births, marriages and deaths – and the key to unlocking the detail they contain is obviously a family surname, one that has been 'inherited' and passed from generation to generation.

No matter our station in life, we all have a surname – but it was not until about the middle of the fourteenth century that the practice of being identified by a particular surname became commonly established throughout the British Isles.

Previous to this, it was normal for a person to be identified through the use of only a forename.

But as population gradually increased and there were many more people with the same forename, surnames were adopted to distinguish one person, or community, from another.

Many common English surnames are patronymic in origin, meaning they stem from the forename of one's father – with 'Johnson,' for example, indicating 'son of John.'

It was the Normans, in the wake of their eleventh century conquest of Anglo-Saxon England, a pivotal moment in the nation's history, who first brought surnames into usage – although it was a gradual process.

For the Normans, these were names initially based on the title of their estates, local villages and chateaux in France to distinguish and identify these landholdings.

Such grand descriptions also helped enhance the prestige of these warlords and generally glorify their lofty positions high above the humble serfs slaving away below in the pecking order who had only single names, often with Biblical connotations as in Pierre and Jacques.

The only descriptive distinctions among the peasantry concerned their occupations, like 'Pierre the swineherd' or 'Jacques the ferryman.'

Roots of surnames that came into usage in England not only included Norman-French, but also Old French, Old Norse, Old English, Middle English, German, Latin, Greek, Hebrew and the Gaelic languages of the Celts.

The Normans themselves were originally Vikings, or 'Northmen', who raided, colonised and eventually settled down around the French coastline.

The had sailed up the Seine in their longboats in 900AD under their ferocious leader Rollo and ruled the roost in north eastern France before sailing over to conquer England in 1066 under Duke William of Normandy – better known to posterity as William the Conqueror, or King William I of England.

Granted lands in the newly-conquered England, some of their descendants later acquired territories in Wales, Scotland and Ireland – taking not only their own surnames, but also the practice of adopting a surname, with them.

But it was in England where Norman rule and custom first impacted, particularly in relation to the adoption of surnames.

This is reflected in the famous *Domesday Book*, a massive survey of much of England and Wales, ordered by William I, to determine who owned what, what it was worth and therefore how much they were liable to pay in taxes to the voracious Royal Exchequer.

Completed in 1086 and now held in the National Archives in Kew, London, 'Domesday' was an Old English word meaning 'Day of Judgement.'

This was because, in the words of one contemporary chronicler, "its decisions, like those of the Last Judgement, are unalterable."

It had been a requirement of all those English landholders – from the richest to the poorest – that they identify themselves for the purposes of the survey and for future reference by means of a surname.

This is why the *Domesday Book*, although written in Latin as was the practice for several centuries with both civic and ecclesiastical records, is an invaluable source for the early appearance of a wide range of English surnames.

Several of these names were coined in connection with occupations.

These include Baker and Smith, while Cooks, Chamberlains, Constables and Porters were to be found carrying out duties in large medieval households.

The church's influence can be found in names such as Bishop, Friar and Monk while the popular name of Bennett derives from the late fifth to mid-sixth century Saint Benedict, founder of the Benedictine order of monks.

The early medical profession is represented by Barber, while businessmen produced names that include Merchant and Sellers.

Down at the village watermill, the names that cropped up included Millar/Miller, Walker and Fuller, while other self-explanatory trades included Cooper, Tailor, Mason and Wright.

Even the scenery was utilised as in Moor, Hill, Wood and Forrest – while the hunt and the chase supplied names that include Hunter, Falconer, Fowler and Fox.

Colours are also a source of popular surnames, as in Black, Brown, Gray/Grey, Green and White, and would have denoted the colour of the clothing the person habitually wore or, apart from the obvious exception of 'Green', one's hair colouring or even complexion.

The surname Red developed into Reid, while

Blue was rare and no-one wanted to be associated with yellow.

Rather self-important individuals took surnames that include Goodman and Wiseman, while physical attributes crept into surnames such as Small and Little.

Many families proudly boast the heraldic device known as a Coat of Arms, as featured on our front cover.

The central motif of the Coat of Arms would originally have been what was borne on the shield of a warrior to distinguish himself from others on the battlefield.

Not featured on the Coat of Arms, but high-lighted on page three, is the family motto and related crest – with the latter frequently different from the central motif.

Adding further variety to the rich cultural heritage that is represented by surnames is the appearance in recent times in lists of the 100 most common names found in England of ones that include Khan, Patel and Singh – names that have proud roots in the vast sub-continent of India.

Echoes of a far distant past can still be found in our surnames and they can be borne with pride in commemoration of our forebears.

Chapter two:

Rebellion and repression

An occupational surname of truly ancient origins, 'Baker' is derived from the Old English *baecere*, indicating a maker or a seller of the staff of life we know as bread.

Early but now redundant forms of the name include Backer, Baiker and Bakere, and the earliest people thought to have first taken up the daily occupation of baking bread were the Egyptians in about 8,000 BC.

In medieval times in England, it was common practice for bread to be baked in a communal oven, normally operated by an employee of the owner of the local manor.

Through time, these 'bakers' became entrepreneurs in their own right – charging a small sum of money to housewives who would bring their already prepared dough to be baked in their ovens.

But some bakers exploited this arrangement by stealing portions of the good housewife's dough, baking it and selling it off as their own.

So widespread was this practice that it eventually led to a regulation known as the Assize of Bread and Ale, which stipulated harsh financial penalties for any baker found to have exploited his customers in such a manner.

To safeguard themselves against any suspicion of impropriety, bakers adopted the custom of baking an extra loaf of bread for every batch – normally in batches of twelve – that they baked.

Hence the well-known phrase 'a baker's dozen', indicating not twelve, but thirteen.

By the very nature of their occupation, bakers were to be found throughout the length and breadth of the British Isles and Ireland – but as 'Baker' became established as a surname, in common with other occupational names, not all of its bearers were necessarily 'bakers.'

A Walter le Baker is recorded in Devon in 1273 and a Jane Baker in London in the mid-sixteenth century – but it is the northern English county of Durham that is particularly identified with early bearers of the name.

It was here, from Crooke Hall and Elemore Hall, that a noted family of Bakers administered considerable landholdings.

But, despite their early association with Durham, it is much further south, in Sussex, that bearers of the Baker name first make an appearance as active participants in the vibrant and frequently bloody drama that is England's history.

This is through Thomas Baker, recognised as one of the leaders of the Peasants' Revolt of 1381.

Also known as the Great Rising or Wat Tyler's Rebellion, the revolt was a significant event in England's history, marking a dramatic turning point in the relationship between the rulers and the ruled.

Although it failed, the harsh lessons learned from it eventually led to slow, albeit reluctant, reform of the feudal system where lords of manors held, literally, the power of life and death over their underlings – keeping them in the state of abject slavery known as serfdom.

But, although known as the Peasants' Revolt, it also had the support of a number of small landholders who objected to the haughty King Richard III's attempt to impose an early form of poll tax to further his costly foreign wars.

The revolt was sparked off in the summer of 1381 in the Essex villages of Brentwood and Fobbing, where Thomas Baker was a small landholder.

When a king's representative attempted to collect the hated poll tax, Baker led the villagers of Brentwood and Fobbing in resisting his demands and accordingly sending the chastened would-be tax collector on his way.

Incensed by this flouting of the royal will, the king despatched Robert Belknap, Chief Justice of the Common Pleas, to the villages to punish his disobedient subjects.

He was promptly attacked by the villagers, led by Baker, and forced to flee.

The revolt swiftly gathered momentum, spreading from Essex into Kent and East Anglia, with the Kentish rebels led by the charismatic Wat Tyler.

As the strength of the rebel forces swelled, they marched on London – assembling at Blackheath on June 12.

Various properties throughout the city were destroyed by the rebels over the next few days, while the Tower of London was stormed and a number of high-ranking officials, including Simon of Sudbury – the Archbishop of Canterbury and Lord Chancellor – summarily beheaded.

It was not until the king in person addressed a gathering of the rebels at Smithfield that the rebellion was defused – with the monarch promising to accede to their demands for reform.

But as the forces dispersed, he quickly reneged on his promises – hastily organising a 700-strong force of militia that hunted down and executed prominent rebel leaders and early champions of democracy who included Wat Tyler and Thomas Baker.

Back to the early Baker heartland of Co. Durham, the family that held manors and estates at Crooke Hall and Elemore Hall branched off into several different geographical directions.

These include the Bakers of Loventor, in Totnes, Devon, who were created Baronets in the Baronetage of Great Britain in 1776, while the Baronetage of the Bakers of Dunstable, Bedfordshire was created in 1796 and that of the Bakers of Ranston, Dorset, in 1802.

But it is the Bakers of Sissinghurst, in Kent, for whom a Baronetage was created in 1611, who have a particularly infamous relevance to English history.

This is through Sir John Baker, the powerful English politician also known as "Bloody Baker" for his ruthless persecution of Protestants during the reign from 1553 to 1558 of Queen Mary I.

Known as the Marian Persecutions, after 'Mary', these particularly bloodthirsty times saw hundreds of Protestant reformers deemed guilty of heresy against the Catholic faith being either sent into exile, imprisoned or burned at the stake.

It was through her role in this persecution that Mary acquired the nickname of "Bloody Mary" – now in more peaceful times the name of a popular alcoholic drink using vodka and tomato juice – while Sir John Baker acquired his of "Bloody Baker."

Born in about 1488, and later serving as both Speaker of the House of Commons and England's first Chancellor of the Exchequer, it was he who first acquired the Sissinghurst estate.

Zealous in his repression of what he deemed as heresy, legend holds that it was in 1558 while he was en route to the village of Cranbrook, in Kent, to oversee the execution of two Protestants, that he received word by messenger that Queen Mary had died.

This is at a spot where three roads meet known to this day as Baker's Cross – and it was from here that he turned back to London, thus inadvertently saving the lives of the two condemned men.

Another legend holds that he was killed on

that fateful day at Baker's Cross – but the truth is that he died some time later in the comfort of his own home.

It was his son, Sir Richard Baker, born in 1528 and who died in 1574, who built Sissinghurst Castle on the family estate while his son, also named Richard, was a famous chronicler of English history.

Born in 1568 and knighted by James I (James VI of Scotland) in 1603, he served as High Sheriff of Oxfordshire before massive debts forced him to seek refuge from his clamouring debtors in London's Fleet Prison.

It was here that he wrote his most noted work, *Chronicle of the Kings of England*, and where he died in 1645.

It had been through another and more financially fortunate relative, Sir Henry Baker, that the Sissinghurst baronetage was created in 1611.

Chapter three:

Spirit of adventure

From as far back as the late fourteenth century Peasants' Revolt, bearers of the Baker name have continued to stamp their mark on the historical record.

One of the physicians to King George III throughout the unfortunate monarch's frequent bouts of mental illness – portrayed in the 1994 film *The Madness of King George* – Sir George Baker was created Baronet Baker of Loventor, in Totnes, Devon, in 1776.

Born in 1722 in Modbury, Devon and elected president of the Royal College of Physicians on no fewer than nine occasions between 1785 and 1795, he not only tended George III but also found a solution to the painful and often fatal condition known as Devonshire Colic.

The condition, Sir George found, was caused by drinking cider in which lead had been used as part of the manufacturing process.

Once lead was removed from the process, the problem was eradicated; he died in 1809.

In common with Sir George Baker, Sir Benjamin Baker is noted in the historical record as an eminent bearer of the name far removed from its original occupational root as a 'baker.'

One of his legacies can be seen to this day in the form of the Forth Railway Bridge, in Scotland, designed and erected by Baker, Sir John Fowler and William Arrol and opened in 1890.

Born in 1840 in Frome, Somerset, the civil and structural engineer also helped to design Egypt's first Aswan Dam, opened in 1902, in addition to collaborating on the design and construction of London's first underground railway system.

Knighted in 1890, he died in 1907.

It is not only in the original Baker heartland of England in particular and the British Isles in general that noted bearers of the name are to be found, but also much further afield.

Of Scots-Irish descent and born in 1818 in Illinois, Jim Baker was a famed frontiersman, trapper, guide and scout of America's Old West.

Known as 'Honest Jim Baker', and a friend and contemporary of other renowned frontiersmen who included Kit Carson and Jim Bridger, it was at the age of 21 that he was hired as a trapper for the

American Fur Company. From then, until his death at the age of 70, his colourful career as a trapper, guide and scout brought him into frequent conflict with Native American tribes such as the Arapaho, Cheyenne, Shoshone and Sioux.

One particularly famous battle in which he was involved was in August of 1841 at Bastion Mountain, in the Rocky Mountains, where his party was attacked by a band of Native Americans.

Under Baker's leadership, they were driven off, and in commemoration of the battle Bastion Mountain was later renamed Battle Mountain.

Despite his many battles with Native Americans, Baker was married six times to women of their tribes – including the daughter of a Cherokee chief and a Shoshone chief, with whom he had a number of children.

He died in 1898 in his cabin near Savery, Wyoming, now rebuilt and relocated at Wyoming's Little Snake River Museum.

In keeping with the adventurous spirit of bearers of the Baker name, Sir Samuel White Baker was the British explorer, big game hunter and writer born in London in 1821, the son of a wealthy banker, ship owner and sugar merchant.

Serving between 1869 and 1873 as British Governor-General of what is now modern-day Northern Uganda and South Sudan, he had previously explored much of Central Africa, while in 1864 he discovered what is now known as Lake Albert while attempting to trace the source of the Nile.

Known as "The White Pasha", he died in 1893, the recipient of many awards and honours that include election as a Fellow of the Royal Society and of the Royal Geographical Association.

His many writings include *In the Heart of Africa*, published in 1886 and his 1891 *True Tales for My Grandsons*.

Another adventurous bearer of the Baker name – but one who came to a particularly horrific end – was the Methodist minister and missionary Thomas Baker.

Born in 1832 in Playden, Sussex, the son of a carpenter, his family immigrated to New South Wales when he was aged seven.

Confirmed as a minister in 1859, he was later despatched as a missionary to Fiji, settling there with his wife.

It was in July of 1867 that, while engaged in

missionary work in the area of Vita Levu, that he and seven of his party were ambushed by native Fijians.

All eight were killed, 'cooked' in pots of boiling water and then cannibalised.

The axe used to kill them is now on display in the Fijian village of Nabutatau, while another gruesome relic, in display in the Fiji Museum in Suva, is the hapless Thomas Baker's boiled shoe.

Bearers of the Baker name have been prominent in the often cut-throat world of politics.

Born in 1934 in Newport, Monmouthshire, Kenneth Baker is the British Conservative Party politician who in 1997 was elevated to the Peerage of the United Kingdom as Baron Baker of Dorking, in East Sussex.

The son of a civil servant, the veteran politician has held a number of political posts.

These include chairman of the Conservative party from 1989 to 1990 under Prime Minister Margaret Thatcher and, from 1990 to 1992, Home Secretary under John Major.

Other posts include Secretary of State for Education and Science and Secretary of State for the Environment.

In American politics, James Baker is the

former Republican Party politician who was presented with the Woodrow Wilson Award for public service in 2000.

Born in 1930 in Houston, Texas, top government positions he held before retiring from active politics include Secretary of the Treasury from 1985 to 1988 under President Ronald Reagan and, from 1989 to 1992, Secretary of State under President George H.W. Bush.

From party politics to political activism, Eric Baker, born in 1920, was the British co-founder in 1961 of the human rights group Amnesty International and also a founder of the Campaign for Nuclear Disarmament (CND).

Responsible for coining Amnesty International's term "prisoner of conscience", he died in 1976.

Chapter four:

On the world stage

Ranked by the American Film Institute as the sixth greatest female star of all time, Norma Jeane Baker was the model, actress and singer better known to posterity as Marilyn Monroe.

Born in Los Angeles in 1926, the name recorded on her birth certificate is Norma Jeane Mortenson, the surname of the man reputed to have been her father, but her mother Gladys (neé Monroe) later insisted that her daughter be known as Norma Jeane Baker.

Complicating matters somewhat, 'Baker' was the surname of Gladys' first husband.

It was as 'Marilyn Monroe' that Norma Jeane Baker, at the age of 20, signed her first film contract with Twentieth Century Fox.

She became an international sex symbol through a number of films of the 1950s and 1960s, famed for her performances both as an actress and a singer in the 1950 *The Asphalt Jungle*, the 1953 *Gentlemen Prefer Blondes*, the 1959 *Some Like it Hot*, and others.

Dogged by illness and other personal problems, she died in August of 1962 from an overdose of barbiturates – by which time she had already become firmly established as a major cultural icon.

Another international sex symbol of the 1950s and 1960s is the American actress **Carroll Baker**, born in 1931 in Johnstown, Pennsylvania.

She first rose to fame in films that include the 1953 *Easy to Love*, the 1958 *The Big Country* and, from 1964, *The Carpetbaggers*.

Also known for films that include the 1979 *The World is Full of Married Men* and the recipient of a star on the Hollywood Walk of Fame, her 1983 autobiography is *Baby Doll*.

The recipient of an MBE for his services to the acting profession, **George Baker** was the English actor and writer born in 1931 in Varna, Bulgaria, where his father was honorary British vice consul.

Best known for his portrayal of Tiberius in the acclaimed 1970 British television drama series *I, Claudius*, and as Inspector Wexford in the 1987 to 2000 television series *The Ruth Rendell Mysteries* – in which his wife, the late actress Louie Ramsay, played his on-screen wife – he died in 2011.

Also on the television screen, **Tom Baker**,

born in Liverpool in 1934, is the English actor best known for his role from 1974 to 1981 as the fourth 'incarnation' of 'The Doctor' in the long-running *Doctor Who* series.

The narrator on both the radio and television series of the comedy *Little Britain*, a survey of British adults in 2005 showed his voice to be the fourth most recognisable after the Queen and politicians Tony Blair and Margaret Thatcher.

Still with the popular *Doctor Who* series, **Colin Baker** is the actor who, from 1984 to 1986, played the sixth 'incarnation' of 'The Doctor.'

Born in London in 1943, he is also known for his role in the 1970s as Paul Merroney in the television series *The Brothers*, while film credits include the 1999 *The Harpist* and the 2000 *The Asylum*.

Formerly married to the English actress Liza Goddard, he is the author of books that include his 2009 *Look Who's Talking*.

From British to American television screens, **Diane Baker** is the actress best known for her roles in shows that include *Bonanza*, *Route 66* and *The Fugitive*.

Born in Hollywood in 1938, her film credits include the 1959 *The Diary of Anne Frank* and the 1964 Alfred Hitchcock film *Marnie*.

Only 3ft. 8in. in height, **Kenny Baker** is the British actor and musician best known as 'the man inside' R2-D2 in the *Star Wars* series of movies.

Born in Birmingham in 1934, his other film credits include *Labyrinth* and *Time Bandits*.

With film credits that include the James Bond *The Living Daylights*, *GoldenEye* and *Tomorrow Never Dies*, **Joe Don Baker** is the American actor born in 1936 in Groesbeck, Texas.

Best known for his role as Patrick Jane in the CBS television series *The Mentalist*, **Simon Baker** is the award-winning Australian actor and director born in 1969 in Launceston, Tasmania.

Married to the actress Rebecca Rigg, his big screen credits include the 1997 *L.A. Confidential*, the 2006 *The Devil Wears Prada* and the 2011 *Margin Call*.

Back to British shores, **Richard Baker** is the eminent broadcaster best known as a newsreader from 1959 to 1982 for BBC News.

Born in 1925 in Willesden, North London, his popular radio shows included *Baker's Dozen* and, on BBC Radio 4, *Start the Week*.

Born in 1957 in Deptford, South London, **Danny Baker** is not only a popular British radio broadcaster but also a comedy writer, screenwriter and journalist.

In a much earlier era of popular entertainment, **Al Baker** was the professional magician, inventor and author whose many 'tricks' included his *Dictionary Test* and *Baker Slates*.

Born in Poughkeepsie, New York, in 1874, he was for many years one of the owners of a famed magic shop in New York's Times Square.

Author of books that include *Magical Ways and Means* and *Mental Magic*, he served as Dean of the Society of American Magicians from 1941 until his death in 1951.

Bearers of the Baker name have also excelled, and continue to excel, in the highly competitive world of sport.

Elected into the Baseball Hall of Fame in 1955, John Franklin Baker was the legendary third baseman born in 1886 in Trappe, Maryland, and better known as **Home Run Baker**.

A player in Major League Baseball from 1908 to 1922 with the Philadelphia Athletics when the team won the 1910, 1911 and 1913 World Series, he died in 1963.

In contemporary baseball, **Dusty Baker**, born

in 1949 in Riverside, California, is the former outfielder who, over a career spanning nearly twenty years, played for teams that include the Atlanta Braves and Los Angeles Dodgers; teams he has managed included the San Francisco Giants and the Cincinnati Reds.

On the fields of European football, **George Baker** is the former Wales international winger and centre forward of the late 1950s, who was born in 1936, while **Joe Baker**, was an England international footballer and club manager.

Although born in Liverpool in 1940, he spent most of his childhood in Motherwell, Scotland, and played club football for teams that include Hibernian, Raith Rovers and Albion Rovers, whom he managed in the early to mid-1980s; he died in 2003.

In American football, **Al "Bubba" Baker** is the former leading defensive linesman, born in 1956 in Jacksonville, Florida, who played in the National Football League (NFL) for teams that include the Detroit Lions, Cleveland Browns and St Louis Cardinals.

From American football to tennis, **Brian Baker**, born in 1985 in Nashville, Tennessee, is the professionally ranked American player who in 2012 reached the fourth round of Wimbledon.

Taking up the game at the tender age of four, **Jamie Baker** is the professional tennis player, born in Glasgow in 1986, who reached the quarter-finals of Junior Wimbledon in 2004 and also in the same year won the 18-and-under British National Championship.

In the fast and often highly dangerous sport of motorsport, **Buddy Baker**, born in 1941 in Florence, South Carolina, is the leading National Association for Stock Car Racing (NASCAR) driver who was named in 1998 as one of NASCAR'S Greatest Drivers.

An inductee of the International Motorsports Hall of Fame, he is the son of the NASCAR Championship Hall of Fame member **Buck Baker**, born in 1919 in Richburg, South Carolina, and who died in 2002.

From sport to music, Peter Edward Baker is the drummer better known as **Ginger Baker**.

Born in 1939 in Lewisham, South London, he is best known – along with Jack Bruce and Eric Clapton – as a member of the 1960s rock band Cream, whose hit albums include the 1966 *Fresh Cream* and the 1967 *Disraeli Gears*.

The recipient of a star on the Hollywood Walk of Fame and a Legend Award from the 2010 Soul Music Awards, **Anita Baker** is the American singer and songwriter born in 1958 in Toledo, Ohio.

Her many other awards include a 1986 Grammy Award for Best R. and B. Vocal Performance for her album *Rapture*, while other top-selling albums include her 2004 *My Everything*.

Born in Bethnal Green, London, in 1954, Rita Maria Cruddington is the singer and television presenter better known as **Cheryl Baker**.

As a member of the band Brotherhood of Man, she represented the United Kingdom at the 1978 Eurovision Song Contest – ending in eleventh place – while three years later, with Buck's Fizz and the song *Making Your Mind Up*, the U.K. was placed first.

An inductee of the Big Band and Jazz Hall of Fame, **Chet Baker** was the American jazz trumpeter and singer, known for albums that include *Chet Baker Sings*. Born in 1929 in Yale, Oklahoma, he died in 1988.

One particularly wealthy and eccentric bearer of the proud name of Baker was the American financier and philanthropist **George Fisher Baker**.

Born in 1840 in Troy, New York, he

left school at the age of 16 to become one of the richest men of his era in the United States.

The son of a shoe-shop owner, his career began as a junior clerk in the New York State Banking Department.

Eventually the director of no fewer than 22 corporations, it was in 1924 that he donated $5m to help to found the renowned centre of academic excellence known as the Harvard Business School – in addition to providing funding for a wide range of charitable causes throughout New York City.

Two years before his death in 1931, he commissioned the manufacture of a special Pierce-Arrow automobile for his daughter's wedding.

With no expense spared, he stipulated the vehicle's roof line be at least five inches higher than standard models.

This was to enable him to comfortably wear his top hat as he accompanied the bride-to-be in the opulent vehicle to her wedding.

It was not until 1978 that the Pierce-Arrow was rediscovered in a barn in Ohio – complete with perfume dispensers and an intercom fashioned from 24 carat gold.